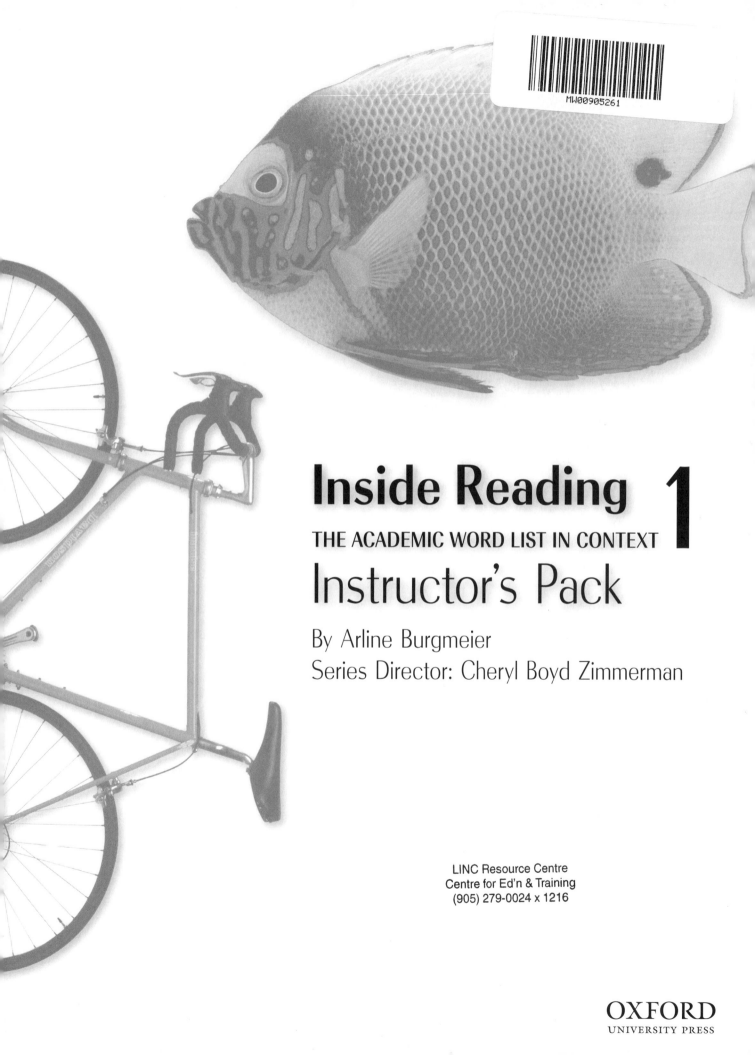

# Inside Reading 1

### THE ACADEMIC WORD LIST IN CONTEXT

## Instructor's Pack

By Arline Burgmeier

Series Director: Cheryl Boyd Zimmerman

**OXFORD**
UNIVERSITY PRESS

# OXFORD
UNIVERSITY PRESS

198 Madison Avenue
New York, NY 10016 USA

Great Clarendon Street, Oxford OX2 6DP UK

Oxford University Press is a department of the University of Oxford.
It furthers the University's objective of excellence in research, scholarship,
and education by publishing worldwide in

Oxford   New York

Auckland   Cape Town   Dar es Salaam   Hong Kong   Karachi
Kuala Lumpur   Madrid   Melbourne   Mexico City   Nairobi
New Delhi   Shanghai   Taipei   Toronto

With offices in

Argentina   Austria   Brazil   Chile   Czech Republic   France   Greece
Guatemala   Hungary   Italy   Japan   Poland   Portugal   Singapore
South Korea   Switzerland   Thailand   Turkey   Ukraine   Vietnam

OXFORD and OXFORD ENGLISH are registered trademarks of
Oxford University Press.

Editorial Director: Sally Yagan
Senior Managing Editor: Patricia O'Neill
Editor: Dena Daniel
Associate Development Editor: Olga Christopoulos
Art Director: Robert Carangelo
Design Manager: Maj-Britt Hagsted
Production Artist: Julie Armstrong
Compositor: TSI Graphics Inc.
Cover design: Stacy Merlin
Manufacturing Manager: Shanta Persaud
Manufacturing Controller: Eve Wong

Instructor's Pack
ISBN: 978 0 19 441620 7
Answer Key Booklet
ISBN: 978 0 19 441601 6

Printed in Hong Kong

10  9  8  7  6  5  4  3  2  1

# Contents

# To the Teacher

There is a natural relationship between academic reading and word learning. *Inside Reading* is a four-level reading and vocabulary series designed to use this relationship to best advantage. Through principled instruction and practice with reading strategies and skills, students will increase their ability to comprehend reading material. Likewise, through a principled approach to the complex nature of vocabulary knowledge, learners will better understand how to make sense of the complex nature of academic word learning. *Inside Reading 1* is intended for students at the low-intermediate level.

## Academic Reading and Vocabulary: A Reciprocal Relationship

In the beginning stages of language learning, when the learner is making simple connections between familiar oral words and written forms, vocabulary knowledge plays a crucial role. In later stages, such as those addressed by *Inside Reading*, word learning and reading are increasingly interdependent: rich word knowledge facilitates reading, and effective reading skills facilitate vocabulary comprehension and learning.[1]

The word knowledge that is needed by the reader in this reciprocal process is more than knowledge of definitions.[2] Truly knowing a word well enough to use it in reading (as well as in production) means knowing something about its grammar, word forms, collocations, register, associations, and a great deal about its meaning, including its connotations and multiple meanings.[3] Any of this information may be called upon to help the reader make the inferences needed to understand the word's meaning in a particular text. For example, a passage's meaning can be controlled completely by a connotation

She was *frugal*. (positive connotation)

She was *stingy*. (negative connotation)

by grammatical form

He valued his *memory*.

He valued his *memories*.

or an alternate meaning

The *labor* was intense. (physical work vs. childbirth)

*Inside Reading* recognizes the complexity of knowing a word. Students are given frequent and varied practice with all aspects of word knowledge. Vocabulary activities are closely related in topic to the reading selections, providing multiple exposures to a word in actual use and opportunities to work with its meanings, grammatical features, word forms, collocations, register, and associations.

To join principled vocabulary instruction with academic reading instruction is both natural and effective. *Inside Reading* is designed to address the reciprocal relationship between reading and vocabulary and to use it to help students develop academic proficiency.

## A Closer Look at Academic Reading

Students preparing for academic work benefit from instruction that includes attention to the language as well as attention to the process of reading. The Interactive Reading model indicates that reading is an active process in which readers draw upon *top-down processing* (bringing meaning to the text), as well as *bottom-up processing* (decoding words and other details of language).[4]

The *top-down* aspect of this construct suggests that reading is facilitated by interesting and relevant reading materials that activate a range of knowledge in a reader's mind, knowledge that is refined and extended during the act of reading.

The *bottom-up* aspect of this model suggests that the learner needs to pay attention to language proficiency, including vocabulary. An academic reading course must address the teaching of higher-level reading strategies without neglecting the need for language support.[5]

---

[1] Koda, 2005

[2] See the meta-analysis of L1 vocabulary studies by Stahl & Fairbanks, 1986.

[3] Nation, 1990

[4] Carrell, Devine and Eskey, 1988

[5] Birch, 2002; Eskey, 1988

*Inside Reading* addresses both sides of the interactive model. High-interest academic readings and activities provide students with opportunities to draw upon life experience in their mastery of a wide variety of strategies and skills, including

- previewing
- scanning
- using context clues to clarify meaning
- finding the main idea
- summarizing
- making inferences.

Rich vocabulary instruction and practice that targets vocabulary from the Academic Word List (AWL) provide opportunities for students to improve their language proficiency and their ability to decode and process vocabulary.

## A Closer Look at Academic Vocabulary

Academic vocabulary consists of those words which are used broadly in all academic domains, but are not necessarily frequent in other domains. They are words in the academic register that are needed by students who intend to pursue higher education. They are not the technical words used in one academic field or another (e.g., *genetics, fiduciary, proton*), but are found in all academic areas, often in a supportive role (*substitute, function, inhibit*).

The most principled and widely accepted list of academic words to date is The Academic Word List (AWL), compiled by Averil Coxhead in 2000. Its selection was based on a corpus of 3.5 million words of running text from academic materials across four academic disciplines: the humanities, business, law, and the physical and life sciences. The criteria for selection of the 570 word families on the AWL was that the words appear frequently and uniformly across a wide range of academic texts, and that they not appear among the first 2000 most common words of English, as identified by the General Service List.[6]

Across the four levels of *Inside Reading*, students are introduced to the 570 word families of the AWL at a gradual pace of about 15 words per unit. Their usage is authentic, the readings in which they appear are high interest, and the words are practiced and recycled in a variety of activities, facilitating both reading comprehension and word learning.

There has been a great deal of research into the optimal classroom conditions for facilitating word learning. This research points to several key factors.

**Noticing:** Before new words can be learned, they must be noticed. Schmidt, in his well-known *noticing hypothesis*, states

> noticing is the necessary and sufficient condition for converting input into intake. Incidental learning, on the other hand, is clearly both possible and effective when the demands of a task focus attention on what is to be learned.[7]

*Inside Reading* facilitates noticing in two ways. Target words are printed in boldface type at their first occurrence to draw the students' attention to their context, usage, and word form. Students are then offered repeated opportunities to focus on them in activities and discussions. *Inside Reading* also devotes activities and tasks to particular target words. This is often accompanied by a presentation box giving information about the word, its family members, and its usage.

Teachers can further facilitate noticing by pre-teaching selected words through "rich instruction," meaning instruction that focuses on what it means to know a word, looks at the word in more than one setting, and involves learners in actively processing the word.[8] *Inside Reading* facilitates rich instruction by providing engaging activities that use and spotlight target words in both written and oral practice.

**Repetition:** Word learning is incremental. A learner is able to pick up new knowledge about a word with each encounter. Repetition also assists learner memory—multiple exposures at varying intervals dramatically enhance retention.

Repetition alone doesn't account for learning; the types and intervals of repetitions are also important.

---

6  West, 1953; Coxhead 2000
7  Schmidt, 1990, p. 129
8  Nation, 2001, p. 157

Research shows that words are best retained when the practice with a new word is brief but the word is repeated several times at increasing intervals.[9] *Inside Reading* provides multiple exposures to words at varying intervals and recycles vocabulary throughout the book to assist this process.

**Learner involvement:** Word-learning activities are not guaranteed to be effective simply by virtue of being interactive or communicative. Activities or tasks are most effective when learners are most *involved* in them. Optimal involvement is characterized by a learner's own perceived need for the unknown word, the desire to search for the information needed for the task, and the effort expended to compare the word to other words. It has been found that the greater the level of learner involvement, the better the retention.[10]

The activities in *Inside Reading* provide opportunities to be involved in the use of target words at two levels:

- "Word level," where words are practiced in isolation for the purpose of focusing on such aspects as meaning, derivation, grammatical features, and associations.
- "Sentence level," where learners respond to the readings by writing and paraphrasing sentences.

Because the activities are grounded in the two high-interest readings of each unit, they provide the teacher with frequent opportunities to optimize learner involvement.

**Instruction and practice with varying types of word knowledge:** To know a word means to know a great deal about the word.[11] The activities in this book include practice with all aspects of word knowledge: form (both oral and written), meaning, multiple meanings, collocations, grammatical features, derivatives, register, and associations.

**Helping students become independent word learners:** No single course or book can address all of the words a learner will need. Students should leave a class with new skills and strategies for word learning so that they can notice and effectively practice new words as they encounter them. *Inside Reading* includes several features to help guide students to becoming independent word learners. One is a self-assessment activity, which begins and ends each unit. Students evaluate their level of knowledge of each word, ranging from not knowing a word at all, to word recognition, and then to two levels of word use. This exercise demonstrates the incremental nature of word knowledge, and guides learners toward identifying what they know and what they need to know. Students can make better progress if they accurately identify the aspects of word knowledge they need for themselves. Another feature is the use of references and online resources: To further prepare students to be independent word learners, instruction and practice in dictionary use and online resources are provided throughout the book.

## The *Inside Reading* Program

*Inside Reading* offers students and teachers helpful ancillaries:

**Student CD-ROM:** The CD-ROM in the back of every student book contains additional practice activities for students to work with on their own. The activities are self-correcting and allow students to redo an activity as many times as they wish.

**Instructor's pack:** The Instructor's Pack contains the answer key for the book along with a test generator CD-ROM. The test generator contains one test per student book unit. Each test consists of a reading passage related to the topic of the unit, which features the target vocabulary. This is followed by reading comprehension and vocabulary questions. Teachers can use each unit's test in full or customize it in a variety of ways.

*Inside Reading* optimizes the reciprocal relationship between reading and vocabulary by drawing upon considerable research and many years of teaching experience. It provides the resources to help students read well and to use that knowledge to develop both a rich academic vocabulary and overall academic language proficiency.

---

[9]  Research findings are inconclusive about the number of repetitions that are needed for retention. Estimates range from 6 to 20. See Nation, 2001, for a discussion of repetition and learning.

[10]  Laufer & Hulstijn, 2001

[11]  Nation, 1990; 2001

# References

Carrel, P.L., Devine, J., & Eskey, D.E. (1988). *Interactive approaches to second language reading*. Cambridge: Cambridge University Press. (Or use "Holding in the bottom" by Eskey)

Coxhead, A. (2000). A new academic word list. *TESOL Quarterly, 34*, 213-238.

Eskey, D.E. (1988). Holding in the bottom. In P.L. Carrel, J. Devine, & D.E. Eskey, *Interactive approaches to second language reading*, pp. 93-100. Cambridge: Cambridge University Press.

Koda, K. (2005). *Insights into second language reading*. Cambridge: Cambridge University Press.

Laufer, B. (2005). Instructed second language vocabulary learning: The fault in the 'default hypothesis'. In A. Housen & M. Pierrard (Eds.), *Investigations in Instructed Second Language Acquisition*, pp. 286-303. New York: Mouton de Gruyter.

Laufer, B. (1992). Reading in a foreign language: How does L2 lexical knowledge interact with the reader's general academic ability? *Journal of Research in Reading, 15*(2), 95-103.

Nation, I.S.P. (1990). *Teaching and learning vocabulary*. New York: Newbury House.

Nation, I.S.P. (2001). *Learning vocabulary in another language*. Cambridge: Cambridge University Press.

Schmidt, R. (1990). The role of consciousness in second language learning. *Applied Linguistics, 11*, 129-158.

Schmitt, N. (2000). *Vocabulary in language teaching*. Cambridge: Cambridge University Press.

Schmitt, N. & Zimmerman, C.B. (2002). Derivative word forms: What do learners know? *TESOL Quarterly, 36*(2), 145-171.

Stahl, S.A. & Fairbanks, M.M. (1986). The effects of vocabulary instruction: A model-based meta-analysis. *Review of Educational Research, 56*(1), 72-110.

# Welcome to *Inside Reading*

*Inside Reading* is a four-level series that develops students' abilities to interact with and access academic reading and vocabulary, preparing them for success in the academic classroom.

There are ten units in *Inside Reading*. Each unit features two readings on a high-interest topic from an academic content area, one or more reading skills and strategies, and work with a set of target word families from the **Academic Word List**.

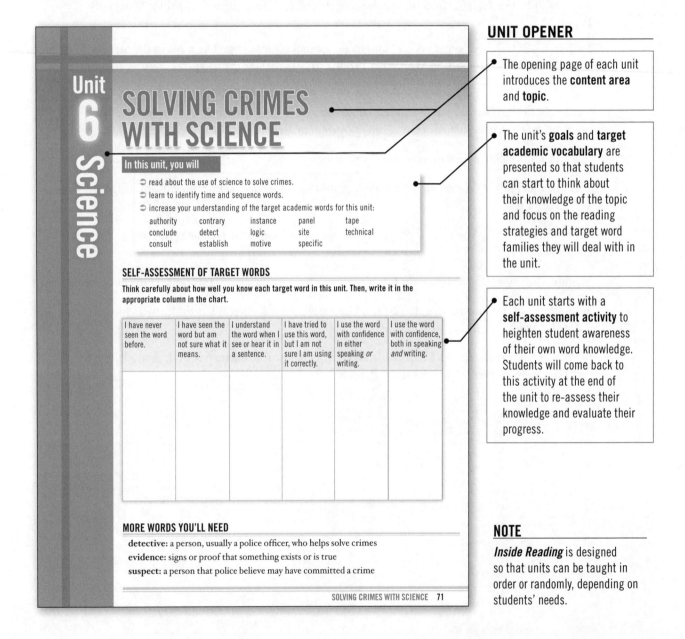

## UNIT OPENER

The opening page of each unit introduces the **content area** and **topic**.

The unit's **goals** and **target academic vocabulary** are presented so that students can start to think about their knowledge of the topic and focus on the reading strategies and target word families they will deal with in the unit.

Each unit starts with a **self-assessment activity** to heighten student awareness of their own word knowledge. Students will come back to this activity at the end of the unit to re-assess their knowledge and evaluate their progress.

## NOTE

*Inside Reading* is designed so that units can be taught in order or randomly, depending on students' needs.

---

*Text within the image:*

**Unit 6 Science**

## SOLVING CRIMES WITH SCIENCE

**In this unit, you will**

- read about the use of science to solve crimes.
- learn to identify time and sequence words.
- increase your understanding of the target academic words for this unit:

| authority | contrary | instance | panel | tape |
| conclude | detect | logic | site | technical |
| consult | establish | motive | specific | |

### SELF-ASSESSMENT OF TARGET WORDS

Think carefully about how well you know each target word in this unit. Then, write it in the appropriate column in the chart.

| I have never seen the word before. | I have seen the word but am not sure what it means. | I understand the word when I see or hear it in a sentence. | I have tried to use this word, but I am not sure I am using it correctly. | I use the word with confidence in either speaking *or* writing. | I use the word with confidence, both in speaking *and* writing. |
|---|---|---|---|---|---|
| | | | | | |

### MORE WORDS YOU'LL NEED

**detective:** a person, usually a police officer, who helps solve crimes

**evidence:** signs or proof that something exists or is true

**suspect:** a person that police believe may have committed a crime

SOLVING CRIMES WITH SCIENCE **71**

## READING 1

### BEFORE YOU READ

Read these questions. Discuss your answers in a small group.

1. Do you ever watch crime stories on television? If so, which one is your favorite?
2. Why do you think people like movies, TV programs, or books about solving crimes?
3. What are some ways that science can help the police solve crimes?

### READ

This newspaper article tells the story of how the police solved the case of a mysterious death.

### Solving a Crime with Science: A True Story

On the morning of June 11, 1986, Sue Snow woke up with a headache. She took two Extra-Strength Excedrin capsules and within minutes she collapsed to the floor. She was rushed to a hospital, but died hours later.

Doctors were unable to explain Sue's death. They asked the hospital laboratory to do some tests to **establish** the cause. One test **detected** cyanide, a poison that can rapidly kill a person who swallows even a small amount. The hospital immediately called the police. They began their investigation by interviewing members of Sue's family.

Mrs. Snow's daughter recalled that her mother had a headache the morning she died and that she had taken two Extra-Strength Excedrin capsules. When a police laboratory subsequently

the two **sites** but learned nothing. Through the media, they warned people about the poisoned medicine and asked them to phone if they had any useful information.

Six days after Sue Snow's death, a woman named Stella Nickell phoned the police to report that her husband, Bruce, had died suddenly on June 5 after taking Extra-Strength Excedrin capsules. When the police searched Stella Nickell's house, they found two bottles of poisoned Extra-Strength Excedrin capsules.

A police detective thought something was very odd. The crime laboratory had tested over 740,000 Extra-Strength Excedrin capsules and found poisoned capsules in only five bottles: two from sites in nearby towns, one in Sue Snow's house and two in Stella Nickell's house. Mrs. Nickell claimed that she had bought her two bottles at two different stores on two different days. **Contrary** to what she claimed,

• Before each of the two readings in a unit, students discuss questions to **activate knowledge of the specific topic** dealt with in the reading.

• Readings represent **a variety of genres**: newspapers, magazines, websites, press releases, encyclopedias, and books.

• Target vocabulary is bold at its first occurrence to aid recognition. **Vocabulary is recycled** and practiced throughout the unit. Target words are also recycled in subsequent units.

## READING COMPREHENSION

Reading comprehension questions follow each text to check students' understanding and recycle target vocabulary.

### READING COMPREHENSION

Mark each sentence as *T* (True) or *F* (False) according to the information in Reading 2. Use your dictionary to check the meaning of new words.

....... 1. Holmes inspected a crime site for anything related to the crime, for instance footprints, broken glass, or hair.

....... 2. CSIs are part of a panel of technical experts in a forensic investigation.

....... 3. Forensic laboratories establish when and where a murder took place by taking hundreds of photographs.

....... 4. To identify footprints, forensic laboratories consult files of footprints of known criminals.

....... 5. CSIs use handheld magnifying glasses to detect trace evidence at crime scenes.

....... 6. Authorities have contrary opinions about using fingerprints for identification.

....... 7. DNA analysis can conclusively establish the motive for a crime.

....... 8. Samples of a suspect's voice can be compared to voice samples from

## READING STRATEGIES

**Strategy presentation and practice** accompanies each reading.

### READING STRATEGY: Identifying Time and Sequence Words

Understanding the *order of events* in a story is often essential for understanding the story, especially a mystery such as Reading 1. The order of events can be shown in several ways:

1. Sentences in a paragraph usually describe actions in the order that they happened.
2. Time words such as *Monday, March, summer*, or *1987* tell when actions took place.
3. Words such as *before, after, soon, first, next, meanwhile, then, finally*, and *subsequently* can show the order of events.
4. Phrases such as *three days later, the next year*, and *at the same time* also show time order.

**A. Use time clues in the reading to determine the date of each of these events.**

Sue Snow died .............................................................................................

Bruce Nickell died ........................................................................................

Stella Nickell phoned the police .....................................................................

## VOCABULARY ACTIVITIES

The vocabulary work following each reading **starts at word level**. Step I activities are mostly receptive and focus on meanings and word family members.

### STEP I VOCABULARY ACTIVITIES: Word Level

**A. Use the target vocabulary in the box to complete this story. The words in parentheses can help you.**

| | | |
|---|---|---|
| abandon | expand | inclined |
| acknowledges | generations | rejecting |
| albeit | in contrast | |

The people of past ............................ ate in restaurants only on weekends or
(1. *people born at about the same time*)
special occasions. ............................, people today are ............................ to eat
(2. *showing a difference*)    (3. *likely*)
out several times a week. This could be a problem if their menu choice is always a
hamburger and French fries. Nearly everyone ............................ that too much
(4. *agrees that it's true*)
fat in the diet is not healthy. Unfortunately, hamburgers and French fries are high
in fat, ............................ delicious. Instead of ............................ fast food
(5. *although*)    (6. *refusing*)
altogether, people should simply ............................ the burgers and fries and
(7. *stop having*)
............................ their food choices by ordering something different.
(8. *increase*)

Vocabulary work then **progresses to the sentence level**. Step II activities are mostly productive and feature work with collocations and specific word usage. These activities can also include work with register, associations, connotations, and learner dictionaries.

### STEP II VOCABULARY ACTIVITIES: Sentence Level

To *expand* means "to grow or increase." The noun form is *expansion*. The adjective form is *expansive*. It means "to cover a wide area."

*The **expansion** took nearly a year to complete.*

*People are happy with the **expansive** new parking lot at the store.*

**E. Restate these sentences in your notebook, using the form of *expand* in parentheses.**

1. The McDonald's menu now includes salads. (*has expanded*)
2. By 2002, the network of McDonald's franchises covered 120 foreign countries. (*expansive*)
3. Recently, McDonald's growth has been faster overseas than in the U.S. (*has been expanding*)
4. Many McDonald's franchises have added a children's play yard to increase their appeal to families. (*expand*)

## NOTE

Each unit ends with topics and projects that teachers can use to take the lesson further. This section includes class discussion topics, online research projects, and essay ideas.

# Answer Key

## Riding Through History

### Reading 1

**Reading Comprehension**
1. True
2. False
3. True
4. True
5. False
6. False
7. False
8. True

**Step I Vocabulary Activities: Word Level**

**A.**
1. changed
2. planned
3. other continents
4. next
5. person
6. structure
7. great
8. payment
9. natural
10. hurt, lessen
11. replace
12. main, task

**B.**
1. a
2. f
3. e
4. c
5. b
6. d

**D.**
1. c
2. d
3. a
4. g
5. f
6. b
7. e

The architect, tailor, doctor, and teacher work primarily during the day.
The taxi driver, pilot, and janitor might work nights instead of days.

**Step II Vocabulary Activities: Sentence Level**

**E.**
2. The jet engine revolutionized air travel.
   The jet engine caused a revolutionary change in air travel.
3. Alfred Nobel created a revolution with a new substance that he called dynamite.
   Alfred Nobel created a revolutionary substance that he called dynamite.
4. The discovery of x-rays created a revolution in medical science.
   The revolutionary discovery of x-rays changed medical science.

**F.**
2. chain
3. wheel (two-letter change)
4. seat
5. tire
6. brake
7. ride
8. pedal

**G.**
1. subsequently substituted
2. subsequent substitution
3. subsequent, substituted

### Reading 2

**Reading Comprehension**
1. True
2. True
3. False
4. False
5. False
6. False
7. True
8. True

**Step I Vocabulary Activities: Word Level**

**A.**
1. had a job
2. an inherent
3. alter
4. designed
5. substituted
6. subsequent
7. injured
8. primary
9. minimize
10. framework
11. individual
12. revolutionized

**B.**
2. injury, action
3. minimize, antonym
4. overseas, synonym
5. fee, action
6. primary, antonym
7. job, example
8. subsequently, antonym

**C.**
1. e
2. d
3. a
4. c
5. b

**D.**
A (alterable): the speed of the bicycle, the direction the bicycle turns, the height of the seat, the speed that the wheels turn, the mirrors on the handlebars
U (unalterable): the size of the wheels, the color of the framework, the design of the bicycle

### E.
1. Each boy works individually to make his own car.
2. First each boy designs his car on paper.
3. He wants to individualize his car so it will be special.
4. He can show his individuality in many ways.
5. To build the car, the designer traces his design on a block of wood.
6. On the day of the race, the Boy Scouts roll their cars individually down a sloped board.
7. The judges give individual prizes for the funniest car, the scariest car, and other categories.
8. Every car is a winner. The contest is designed to show every boy's individuality.

## UNIT 2
# Fighting Diseases

## Reading 1
### Reading Comprehension
1. True
2. True
3. False
4. True
5. True
6. True
7. True
8. False
9. False
10. True

### Reading Strategy: Finding the Main Idea
**A.**
The place most intensely affected by malaria is Africa south of the Sahara Desert.
**B.**
a. The beginning of the malaria cycle
**C.**
b. Becoming infected is a medical emergency
**D.**
b. Plans to prevent malaria are difficult to implement

### Step I Vocabulary Activities: Word Level
**A.**
1. c
2. a
3. d
4. b
**B.**
1. d
2. a
3. b
4. e
5. c

### C.
*Answers may vary. Possible answers:*
a broken arm, a heart attack, a high fever
### D.
1 and 3 have conflicting information.

## Step II Vocabulary Activities: Sentence Level
### F.
2. Young children share combs, hats and other headgear, which intensifies the chance that they may pick up head lice from a friend.
3. Parents are sometimes intensely embarrassed when the school informs them that their child has head lice, but it is not their fault.
4. There is intense conflict in some schools about whether children should attend school when they have head lice.
5. The conflict intensifies when some parents send their children to school with head lice, but others keep their child at home when a classmate has lice.
6. The only symptom of head lice is an intense itching of the head.
7. Getting rid of lice requires intensive work.
8. The child's hair must be washed with an intense chemical rinse. The parent must then search for remaining lice eggs and pick them out.

### G.
*Answers may vary. One possible order:*
1. giving medicine to sick people
2. giving food to sick people
3. spraying homes with insecticide
4. getting rid of pools of water
5. cutting down tall grass
6. teaching people to wash their hands

## Reading 2
### Reading Comprehension
1. True
2. False
3. True
4. False
5. True
6. False
7. False
8. True
9. True

### Reading Strategy
*Answers may vary. Possible answers:*
1. Scientists believe that new plants from the rainforests or simple medicines from people

who live there might be sources for future miracle drugs.
2. Four hundred years ago a miracle drug was found to cure malaria.
3. The ancient people of China had used wormwood to cure fevers.
4. Aspirin was first used over 2,000 years ago.
5. Taxol is an example of how miracle drugs are still being found.
6. Access to rainforest plants is rapidly disappearing.
7. Scientists fear that as rainforest species disappear, possible cures for diseases disappear with them.

## Step I Vocabulary Activities: Word Level
**A.**

| | |
|---|---|
| 1. e | 4. b |
| 2. d | 5. f |
| 3. a | 6. c |

**B.**

| | |
|---|---|
| 1. resided | 5. priority |
| 2. accompanied | 6. access |
| 3. occurred | 7. practitioners |
| 4. labored | 8. declined |

**D.**
A (accessible): other children, education, parks, battery-operated toys
I (inaccessible): scissors, electrical toys, stairs, their medicines, the bathroom water faucet

## Step II Vocabulary Activities: Sentence Level
**H.**
*Answers will vary. Possible answers:*
1. How will you implement the new plan to control malaria?
2. Will everyone have access to clinics?
3. Will you build more medical facilities?
4. Do you have plans for residential spraying?
5. Will you ask neighboring countries to cooperate with your efforts?

## UNIT 3
# They Know What You Want

## Reading 1
### Reading Comprehension

| | |
|---|---|
| 1. True | 3. True |
| 2. True | 4. False |

| | |
|---|---|
| 5. True | 7. False |
| 6. False | 8. True |

## Reading Strategy: Scanning
1. 200
2. sex, age, education, income
3. they want their babies to be healthy
4. they want to be good mothers
5. Healthy Start
6. Give your baby a healthy start.
7. they must decide

## Step I Vocabulary Activities: Word Level
**A.**
1. sex, example
2. publish, action
3. export, synonym
4. implicit, antonym
5. administer, synonym
6. income, action

**B.**

| | |
|---|---|
| 1. Surveys | 5. domestic |
| 2. sector | 6. sexism |
| 3. administrators | 7. explicit |
| 4. published | 8. implicit |

**D.**
*Answers may vary. Possible answers:*
2. a high school or college campus
3. a library or bookstore
4. Disneyland
5. a bus, bus stop, or bus depot
6. an airport

## Step II Vocabulary Activities: Sentence Level
**E.**
innovative, innovate, innovator, innovation, innovation, innovate
**F.**
2. They want to convince people to change the way they eat.
3. They have convincing evidence that junk foods are to blame.
4. Food companies advertise convincingly that junk foods are something that people should eat all the time.
5. Children are especially easy to convince.
6. Even if an ad shows something unconvincing, children think it's real information.
7. Food companies are unconvinced that they are to blame for children's obesity.

8. They are unconvinced that the responsibility for a child's diet is their responsibility.

**G.**
2. South Korea Exports 50,686 Cars to Russia in 2004
3. Honda and Toyota Make Japan Top Exporter of Cars
4. Italy Exports Fiats Globally
5. Over Half U.S. Cars Are Exports from Other Countries
6. Volkswagen Germany's Best Export
7. Exporting Saabs to Asia Good for Sweden

## Reading 2

### Reading Comprehension
1. True
2. False
3. True
4. True
5. True
6. False
7. False
8. True

### Reading Strategy
**A.**
1. 5 (Xerox, Rolex, Rolodex, Windex, Lexis)
2. 3 (Aleve, Volvo, Nova)
3. 3 (Energizer, Sleepeez, Mazda)

**B.**
1. cruise line
2. computer
3. pain reliever
4. desk index
5. weight loss product
6. window cleaner
7. breakfast cereal
8. automobile
9. antacid tablets
10. battery

### Step I Vocabulary Activities: Word Level
**A.**
*Answers may vary. Possible answers:*
1. energy bar
2. tomato sauce
3. dictionary
4. toothpaste
5. make up
6. gasoline

**B.**
1. e
2. f
3. a
4. b
5. d
6. c

**C.**
1. sexes
2. sexually
3. explicit
4. explicitly
5. sex
6. implicitly
7. sex
8. implicit
9. implicitly

### Step II Vocabulary Activities: Sentence Level
**D.**
2. Dog lovers think of their pets as family members rather than as domesticated animals.
3. A "white sale" is when domestic products, such as towels, are on sale.
4. You should arrive at the airport two hours before domestic flights.
5. Coffee must be imported because it is not grown domestically.

**E.**
2. Fred Black is the administrator of operations for the entire company.
3. Ellen White's administrative responsibility is marketing.
4. Jane Gray administers the employment office.
5. Jerry Green is responsible for the administration of safety and maintenance.

## UNIT 4
# What Your Clothes Say About You

## Reading 1

### Reading Comprehension
1. True
2. True
3. False
4. False
5. False
6. False
7. False
8. True
9. True
10. False

### Reading Strategy: Identifying Examples
1. Paragraph 3: T-shirts
   Paragraph 4: business suits
   Paragraph 5: uniforms
   Paragraph 6: Scottish tartans, colored headscarves
   Paragraph 7: wedding rings, bonnets
2. a. Another
   b. There are many kinds of
3. military personnel, police officers, fire fighters, medical workers, airline pilots, members of religious orders, judge, chef
4. for example

### Step I Vocabulary Activities: Word Level
**A.**
1. constituted
2. whereby
3. conventional
4. via

5. somewhat
6. context
7. acquired
8. integral

**C.**
1. f
2. d
3. a
4. b
5. c
6. e

**D.**
M (military): captain, general, soldier
R (religious): monk, nun, priest
C (civil): fire fighter, lawyer, librarian, manager

## Step II Vocabulary Activities: Sentence Level

**E.**
differentiated, differentiating, differentiate

**F.**
2. ambiguous word: Flies
   Rare Monkey Flies and Eats Carrots
   Rare Monkey Eats Flies and Carrots
3. ambiguous word: Administers
   Doctor Manages Testing of New Drug
   Doctor Gives New Drug Test to Patients
4. ambiguous word: Miss
   Streetcar Rolls Away Before Bus Riders Get On
   Bus Riders Wish Streetcars Would Return

**G.**
*Answers may vary. Possible answers:*
1. Brides conventionally wear white dresses.
2. The conventional dress for students is jeans and a T-shirt.
3. Students like to convene in the cafeteria.
4. The convention is for people to bow and then shake hands.

**H.**
2. a
3. d
4. c
5. b

## Reading 2

### Reading Comprehension
1. True
2. True
3. False
4. False
5. True
6. True
7. True
8. False

### Reading Strategy
1. Contemporary cultures employ many common things, including clothing, as symbols of social status.
2. Paragraph 2: judges
   Paragraph 3: kings and queens
   Paragraph 4: graduates

Paragraph 6: brides
Paragraph 7: religious leaders
Paragraph 8: military personnel
3. capes, crowns, scepters
4. long white gown, white veil, bouquet of flowers
5. One type, and another, A third type
6. First, Second, Finally

## Step I Vocabulary Activities: Word Level

**A.**
1. c
2. g
3. d
4. b
5. a
6. e
7. f

**B.**
*Answers may vary. Possible answers:*
1. good nutrition, inherited long life, good health care services, etc.
2. strong educational system, respect for learning, inexpensive college tuition, etc.
3. strong economy, healthy industries, strong work ethic, etc.
4. trust in government, easy access to polls, belief in democracy, etc.

**C.**
1. a long robe (or head covering)
2. tassel
3. rings
4. a white wedding dress

## Step II Vocabulary Activities: Sentence Level

**D.**
*Answers may vary. Possible answers:*
2. in the context of a battle
3. in a ceremonial context
4. in the context of the kitchen

---

**UNIT 5**

# Success Story

## Reading 1

### Reading Comprehension
1. False
2. True
3. True
4. False
5. True
6. False
7. True
8. True
9. True

## Reading Strategy: Identifying Definitions
1. the energy that drives people to work hard, to learn more, and to seek opportunities to advance themselves
2. the ability to focus on a task despite interruptions, obstacles, and setbacks
3. stop
4. those who take effective action to make things happen
5. take advantage of

## Step I Vocabulary Activities: Word Level
**A.**

| | |
|---|---|
| 1. dominant | 6. dynamic |
| 2. professional | 7. demonstrated |
| 3. attained | 8. positive |
| 4. coincided with | 9. generating |
| 5. was aware | |

**B.**

| | |
|---|---|
| 1. d | 4. e |
| 2. b | 5. a |
| 3. f | 6. c |

**C.**
Correct: fear of failure, fear of being laughed at

**D.**
N (new media): the Internet, magazines, newspapers, radio, television
P (print media): books, magazines, newspapers
A (advertising media): the Internet, magazines, newspapers, radio, television

**E.**
*Answers may vary. Possible answers:*
1. laughter/happy feelings/happiness
2. sales/profits/income/money
3. programs/software
4. plans/designs

## Step II Vocabulary Activities: Sentence Level
**F.**
2. a
   Possible new sentence: It was a coincidence that both Sam and his friend Judith were on the same bus.
3. b
   Possible new sentence: It is coincidental that Sue and Lou both have birthdays on June 1, and that their names rhyme.
4. b
   Possible new sentence: By coincidence, all of the players on the basketball team are named Brown.

**G.**

| | |
|---|---|
| 1. dominant | 3. dominance/ domination |
| 2. dominate | 4. dominates |

# Reading 2
## Reading Comprehension

| | |
|---|---|
| 1. True | 5. False |
| 2. True | 6. True |
| 3. False | 7. False |
| 4. True | 8. False |

## Reading Strategy
**A.**
1. very important and special
2. very ordinary people
3. exploit others
4. attention, everyone
5. great charm
6. talk about themselves
7. the conversation
8. their talents and personal achievements
9. Lying
10. satisfy his needs and admire him
11. everything else in their lives

## Step I Vocabulary Activities: Word Level
**A.**

| | |
|---|---|
| 1. B | 6. B |
| 2. P | 7. B |
| 3. B | 8. B |
| 4. B | 9. P |
| 5. A | |

**C.**

| | |
|---|---|
| 1. helpful | 2. approving |

**D.**

| | |
|---|---|
| 1. obtained | 3. attained |
| 2. attained | 4. obtained |

A (attainable): a high school diploma, a well-paying job, fluency in a second language, happiness
U (unattainable): a journey to the moon, a Nobel prize, an Olympic gold medal, the command of a naval ship

## Step II Vocabulary Activities: Sentence Level
**E.**

| | |
|---|---|
| 1. N | 3. N |
| 2. P | 4. P |

**F.**

demonstrate, demonstrate, demonstrated, demonstration

**G.**

*Answers may vary. Possible answers:*

1. Ahn went to the United States because the economic slowdown in his home country inhibited his professional opportunities.
2. He was too inhibited to make friends with his colleagues.
3. He wanted to feel more uninhibited when he spoke.
4. His teacher told the students, "You must lose your inhibitions."
5. The teacher understood why the students were inhibited.

---

# Solving Crimes with Science

## Reading 1

### Reading Comprehension

| | | | |
|---|---|---|---|
| 1. False | | 6. False | |
| 2. True | | 7. True | |
| 3. False | | 8. True | |
| 4. False | | 9. False | |
| 5. False | | 10. False | |

### Reading Strategy: Identifying Time and Sequence Words

**A.**

Sue Snow died June 11, 1986
Bruce Nickell died June 5, 1986
Stella Nickell phoned police June 17, 1986

**B.**

Correct order:

1. Stella borrowed library books about poisons.
2. Stella created a clever scheme.
3. Stella poisoned 5 bottles of Extra-Strength Excedrin.
4. Stella placed 3 bottles of Extra-Strength Excedrin in nearby stores.
5. Sue Snow bought a bottle of Extra-Strength Excedrin.

### Step I Vocabulary Activities: Word Level

**A.**

*Answers may vary. Possible answers:*

1. a dictionary, an English teacher
2. a telephone directory, the restaurant's web site, an advertisement
3. a travel agent, the airline's web site, an advertisement
4. a cook book, a friend, the label on a package of noodles

**B.**

| | |
|---|---|
| 1. logic | 6. establish |
| 2. consult | 7. specific |
| 3. instance | 8. conclude |
| 4. site | 9. contrary |
| 5. detect | |

**C.**

| | |
|---|---|
| 1. c | 4. b |
| 2. e | 5. a |
| 3. f | 6. d |

### Step II Vocabulary Activities: Sentence Level

**E.**

1. The hospital laboratory established that Sue had been poisoned.
2. The police established that two bottles containing poisoned Excedrin capsules were found in nearby towns.
3. The police established that Bruce Nickell had life insurance that would pay $176,000, if his death were accidental.
4. The detectives established that Stella had borrowed several books about poison.

**F.**

1. The police ask many specific questions, like the victim's name and age.
2. The police need to know the specifics of what happened.
3. They want to know specifically when the crime happened.
4. They want witnesses to specify what they saw.
5. They hope witnesses can give them specific information about the crime.

## Reading 2

### Reading Comprehension

| | | | |
|---|---|---|---|
| 1. True | | 6. False | |
| 2. True | | 7. False | |
| 3. False | | 8. True | |
| 4. False | | 9. True | |
| 5. True | | 10. True | |

## Reading Strategy

**A.**

1. a century ago
2. immediately
3. first

**B.**

2. dust objects for fingerprints
1. take photographs
5. send evidence to a forensic laboratory
7. present their evidence in a court of law
3. look for drops of blood or strands of hair
4. label the evidence
6. consult with the police chief

## Step I Vocabulary Activities: Word Level

**A.**

1. technical assistance
2. technical explanation
3. technical words
4. technical person

**C.**

*Answers may vary. Possible answers:*

1. the coach, the referee
2. the teacher, the principal
3. the police, court official
4. the parents
5. the person's boss
6. the manager/owner

**D.**

1. b      3. d
2. c      4. a

## Step II Vocabulary Activities: Sentence Level

**E.**

1. detector      4. detects
2. detectives      5. detective
3. detectable      6. detection

**F.**

2. c      4. d
3. b      5. a

**G.**

*Answers may vary. Possible answers:*

1. The police came to the conclusion that Linda was guilty.
2. The fingerprints were inconclusive because Jim could have touched the wall days before the theft.
3. Linda's fingerprints proved conclusively that she stole the painting.

## Reading 1

### Reading Comprehension

1. False      6. False
2. True      7. False
3. False      8. True
4. True      9. True
5. True

### Reading Strategy: Reading Numerical Tables

**A.**

1. Jack in the Box, Wendy's
2. Domino's Pizza
3. 7,320

## Step I Vocabulary Activities: Word Level

**A.**

1. generations      5. albeit
2. In contrast      6. rejecting
3. inclined      7. abandon
4. acknowledges      8. expand

**B.**

2. 10 years      4. 1,000 years
3. 100 years      5. 366 days

**C.**

1. f      4. a
2. c      5. d
3. e      6. b

**E.**

1. d      3. b
2. a      4. c

**F.**

1. complement      3. complements
2. complimentary      4. complementary

## Step II Vocabulary Activities: Sentence Level

**G.**

*Answers may vary. Possible answers:*

2. The burger was good, albeit small.
3. The broken chairs in the restaurant contrast with the shiny new tables.
4. A mother and her little boy have contrasting ideas about a good lunch.
5. Cola drinks cost 75¢. In contrast, water is free.
6. There was a big contrast between the cost of the teen-aged girl's tiny salad and her boyfriend's enormous hamburger.

**H.**

*Answers may vary. Possible answers:*

1. abandoned by customers.
2. reject a new food.
3. people rejected them.
4. have to abandon their plans.
5. we abandoned our plans.
6. rejected his offer.

# Reading 2

## Reading Comprehension

1. True
2. False
3. False
4. True
5. True
6. True
7. False

## Reading Strategy

1. Kumon, Dunkin' Donuts, Burger King, Midas, Days Inn, McDonald's, KFC.
2. Kumon, Midas, Dunkin' Donuts and McDonald's, KFC, Burger King, Days Inn.
3. Kumon (smallest); Days Inn (largest).
4. Possible answers: no expensive equipment needed; can set up in any existing office or store; no special furniture needed; no uniforms needed.

## Step I Vocabulary Activities: Word Level

**A.**

1. e
2. d
3. b
4. a
5. c

**B.**

1. generation
2. in contrast
3. had an inclination
4. expanded
5. contemporary
6. output
7. complement
8. grade

**C.**

1. e
2. d
3. c
4. a
5. b

**D.**

(time) Roman History overlaps with Europe from 1850 to Present Day; Europe from 1800–1900 overlaps with The History of China. (subject matter) Roman History overlaps with Roman and Greek History; Europe from 1850 to Present Day overlaps with Europe from 1800–1900.

## Step II Vocabulary Activities: Sentence Level

**E.**

1. The McDonald's menu has expanded to include salads.
2. By 2002, the expansive network of McDonald's franchises covered 120 foreign countries.
3. Recently, McDonald's has been expanding faster overseas than in the U.S.
4. Many McDonald's franchises have added a children's play yard to expand their appeal to families.

**F.**

1. economically
2. economize
3. economy
4. economical
5. Economists
6. economy
7. economic

**G.**

*Answers may vary. Possible answers:*

2. A teenager's eating habits incline toward fast food.
3. People who can't swim are not inclined to own sailboats.
4. Dogs are inclined to bark at strangers.
5. Little sisters are inclined to copy their big sisters.

## UNIT 8
# The Autism Puzzle

## Reading 1

### Reading Comprehension

1. True
2. True
3. True
4. False
5. True
6. False
7. False
8. True
9. True
10. False
11. True

### Reading Strategy: Making Inferences

2. a and c
3. b and c
4. c
5. a and b
6. a and b

### Step I Vocabulary Activities: Word Level

**A.**

1. phases
2. appropriate
3. participate
4. interact
5. task
6. assess
7. capabilities
8. constrain
9. relax
10. mature

**B.**

Correct: a, d, f, g, h, i

**C.**

Correct order:

1. f
2. c
3. b
4. a
5. d
6. e

## Step II Vocabulary Activities: Sentence Level

**E.**

1. assess
2. assessable
3. assessment
4. assesses
5. reassessment
6. reassessed

**F.**

*Sentences may vary. Possible answers:*

2. Shawn can easily take a spelling test. He excels at spelling in school.
3. Shawn will be able to solve subtraction problems because he excels at math.
4. Shawn will have difficulty working with a committee. He doesn't like to interact with others and his language skills are poor.
5. It will be difficult for Shawn to give an oral report. His language skills are poor.

**H.**

*Sentences may vary. Possible answers:*

2. To respond appropriately, Sam should say "Oh, I'd like to." Or "I'm sorry, but I can't."
3. Sam's response is inappropriate. He should say, "Sure. Here it is."
4. Sam's answer is appropriate.

# Reading 2

## Reading Comprehension

1. False
2. True
3. True
4. False
5. True
6. True
7. True

## Reading Strategy

Paragraph 2

1. D
2. D
3. I
4. I
5. I

Paragraph 3

1. I
2. I
3. D
4. N
5. D

Paragraph 4

1. I
2. D
3. I
4. N
5. D

## Step I Vocabulary Activities: Word Level

**A.**

C (capable): listening to music, riding on a bus, telling jokes, using a telephone

I (incapable): driving a car, reading a newspaper

**B.**

2. relax
3. relax it
4. relax it
5. relax

**D.**

1. d
2. f
3. b
4. c
5. a
6. e

## Step II Vocabulary Activities: Sentence Level

**E.**

1. immaturity
2. mature
3. maturation
4. immature
5. maturity
6. maturational

**F.**

*Sentences may vary. Possible answers:*

2. Nouns are the easiest because they are predominantly things you can picture.
3. Verbal thinkers predominate in universities.
4. Dr. Grandin was surprised by the predominance of people who think only in words.
5. Seeing pictures in her mind is the predominant way Temple Grandin creates ideas.

**G.**

*Sentences may vary. Possible answers:*

2. Boys outnumber girls by a ratio of 105 to 100 at birth.
3. Among autistic children, girls are outnumbered by boys by a ratio of 1 to 4.
4. Of adults who are colorblind, men outnumber women 15 to 1.
5. At age 65, women outnumber men by a ratio of 10 to 7.

**H.**

1. participate
2. participants
3. participants
4. participation
5. participating
6. participatory

## UNIT 9
# Sea of Life

## Reading 1
### Reading Comprehension
1. True
2. False
3. True
4. True
5. False
6. True
7. True
8. False
9. False
10. True

### Reading Strategy: Reading Statistical Tables
**B.**
b. I
c. I
d. I
e. I
f. N
g. I
h. N

### Step I Vocabulary Activities: Word Level
**A.**
1. terminate, antonym
2. temporary, example
3. erode, synonym
4. aggregate, part
5. process, part

**B.**
*Answers may vary. Possible answers:*
1. mountains: wind, rain, animals, floods, forest fires
2. soil: floods, animals
3. hopes: lack of money, family objections, not being chosen, too young or old
4. pavement: traffic, freezing, floods, sun
5. enjoyment of movies: In the theater, talking people, cell phones, too cold, crying babies; In the film, too much violence, sound too loud, too long
6. respect for a leader: scandals, lying, poor leadership, breaking law, bad decisions

**C.**
2. a library, a bookstore
3. a garden, a farm, a forest, woods, a park
4. an audience, a mob, a group, a party
5. a book, a newspaper, a magazine

**D.**
Correct: spring, your birthday, New Year's Day, October, animal migrations

**E.**
1. b
2. d
3. e
4. c
5. a

**F.**
1. traced
2. annual
3. compatible
4. impact
5. erosion
6. contributed
7. process
8. ultimately

### Step II Vocabulary Activities: Sentence Level
**H.**
2. Her new job impacted the whole family. Her new job had an impact on the whole family.
3. The collision had a different impact on each of us. The collision impacted each of us differently.
4. The new law will impact the way people pay their taxes. The new law will have an impact on the way people pay their taxes.

**I.**
1. My aunt contributed a used coffee maker.
2. My dad's contribution was a small bookcase.
3. My brother Jim was the contributor of three red pillows.
4. My mom contributed a frying pan.
5. My best friend is contributing three posters.

## Reading 2
### Reading Comprehension
1. True
2. False
3. True
4. False
5. True
6. True
7. False

### Reading Strategy
Length: 23 feet 4 inches
Weight: 37,400 pounds
Maximum depth: 14,764 feet
Maximum speed: 2 knots
Range: 6 miles
Occupants: three
Propulsion: five hydraulic thrusters
Electrical system: lead-acid batteries
Equipment (internal): gyrocompass, magnometer, computer
Equipment (external): viewing lamp, cameras, two arms

## Step I Vocabulary Activities: Word Level

**A.**

Correct: a cut finger, a camping tent, a headache, a substitute teacher, a vacation, a rainstorm

**C.**

1. f
2. a
3. e
4. b
5. d
6. g
7. c

**D.**

1. e
2. d
3. f
4. a
5. b
6. c

## Step II Vocabulary Activities: Sentence Level

**E.**

2. Detectives are conducting a search for the missing murder weapon.
3. Marketers will conduct a survey to identify future customers.
4. A famous composer conducted a local orchestra playing his Symphony in F.
5. Ocean scientists will conduct an experiment on poisonous algae.

**G.**

2. The process of vent formation begins when seawater seeps down into the earth's crust.
3. The seawater is heated to over 750°. In the process, it expands.
4. In the process of rising through the cracks, the hot water dissolves chemicals from the rock.
5. Some of the minerals harden and, in the process, form a rim around the vent.
6. The process happens again and again until a tall chimney forms.

---

**UNIT 10**

# Giving Nature a Hand

## Reading 1

### Reading Comprehension

1. True
2. True
3. False
4. False
5. False
6. True
7. True
8. False

## Reading Strategy: Fact versus Opinion

**A.**

2. Opinion
3. Opinion
4. Fact
5. Fact
6. Opinion

**C.**

It [being toothless] also made them physically unattractive.

## Step I Vocabulary Activities: Word Level

**A.**

1. e
2. b
3. d
4. c
5. a

**B.**

2. ~~I'm angry that~~ taxpayers will face ~~yet~~ another ~~large, unwelcome~~ tax increase.
3. The audience applauded ~~wildly~~ after the ~~best~~ performance ~~I've ever seen.~~
4. Two ~~sweet~~ children ~~from a terrible family~~ were found sleeping in the park.
5. ~~I'm happy to report that~~ the ~~awful~~ man ~~got what he deserved and~~ was arrested.

**C.**

1. impose
2. voluntarily
3. proportion
4. advocate
5. objective
6. incentive
7. alternative
8. tense
9. confined

**E.**

1. c
2. f
3. e
4. a
5. b
6. d

## Step II Vocabulary Activities: Sentence Level

**F.**

Paragraph 2: The history of eyeglasses began many centuries ago.

Paragraph 3: Modern ways to correct vision are different from earlier ways.

*Answers may vary. Possible answers:*

Paragraph 5: To sum up, dentures were uncomfortable and expensive until rubber was used to make modern dentures.

Paragraph 6: In summation, dental implants are permanent replacements for lost teeth.

**H.**

*Answers may vary. Possible answers:*

1. Society discriminates against people who are fat.
2. People who are colorblind usually cannot discriminate between red and green.
3. It is against the law for employers to discriminate against someone because of his race.
4. Immigrants often face discrimination in their new countries.
5. Movie actors wear contact lenses because studios discriminate against actors who wear glasses.
6. I can't discriminate between the taste of lemons and limes.

# Reading 2

## Reading Comprehension

| | | | |
|---|---|---|---|
| 1. | False | 5. | True |
| 2. | True | 6. | True |
| 3. | True | 7. | False |
| 4. | True | 8. | True |

## Reading Strategy

**A.**

| | | | |
|---|---|---|---|
| 1. | Fact | 4. | Fact |
| 2. | Opinion | 5. | Opinion |
| 3. | Opinion | | |

**B.**

She was very brave.

## Step I Vocabulary Activities: Word Level

**B.**

2. a library, confined its children's books, to a cozy corner.
3. a private school, confined its student body, to girls under 18.
4. a clothing store, confined its merchandise, to items under $20.
5. an auto repair shop, confined its repairs, to Japanese cars.
6. a radio station, confined its broadcasting, to ten hours a day.
7. a magazine, confined its articles, to 900 words.

**D.**

| | | | |
|---|---|---|---|
| 1. | d | 4. | c |
| 2. | f | 5. | a |
| 3. | b | 6. | e |

## Step II Vocabulary Activities: Sentence Level

**E.**

*Answers may vary. Possible answers:*

1. The boss suspended our lab technician for a week for being careless.
2. He will not be paid during his suspension.
3. Our school will suspend classes during the summer.
4. Electrical wires were suspended from power poles.
5. To save space, they were going to suspend their bikes from the ceiling.
6. The moon looked like it was suspended right over my house.

**F.**

*Answers may vary. Possible answers:*

2. Food from the sea provides a small proportion of the world's total food supply.
3. A disproportionate number of people rely on fish as a primary source of protein.
4. Ambition seems to be proportional with middle class status.
5. Celebrities are disproportionately narcissistic.
6. There is a disproportionate number of boys with autism.
7. A large proportion of the world's malaria cases occur in sub-Saharan Africa.
8. As the rainforests disappear, a proportional number of native people will also disappear.
9. The number of new gas stations built along the highways was proportional to the number of fast food restaurants that were built.
10. McDonald's had a greater proportion of franchises than Burger King in 2005.

# Inside Reading 1

## The Academic Word List
(words targeted in Level 1 are bold)

| Word | Sublist | Location | Word | Sublist | Location | Word | Sublist | Location |
|------|---------|----------|------|---------|----------|------|---------|----------|
| **abandon** | 8 | **L1, U7** | **attain** | 9 | **L1, U5** | complex | 2 | L4, U2 |
| abstract | 6 | L3, U5 | attitude | 4 | L4, U6 | component | 3 | L4, U3 |
| academy | 5 | L3, U1 | attribute | 4 | L3, U10 | compound | 5 | L4, U6 |
| **access** | 4 | **L1, U2** | author | 6 | L2, U4 | comprehensive | 7 | L2, U7 |
| accommodate | 9 | L2, U7 | **authority** | 1 | **L1, U6** | comprise | 7 | L4, U9 |
| **accompany** | 8 | **L1, U2** | automate | 8 | L3, U6 | compute | 2 | L4, U8 |
| accumulate | 8 | L2, U4 | available | 1 | L3, U5 | conceive | 10 | L4, U10 |
| accurate | 6 | L4, U6 | **aware** | 5 | **L1, U5** | concentrate | 4 | L3, U8 |
| achieve | 2 | L4, U1 | | | | concept | 1 | L3, U1 |
| **acknowledge** | 6 | **L1, U7** | behalf | 9 | L3, U9 | **conclude** | 2 | **L1, U6** |
| **acquire** | 2 | **L1, U4** | benefit | 1 | L4, U2 | concurrent | 9 | L4, U5 |
| adapt | 7 | L4, U7 | bias | 8 | L4, U8 | **conduct** | 2 | **L1, U9** |
| adequate | 4 | L2, U4 | bond | 6 | L4, U3 | confer | 4 | L4, U4 |
| adjacent | 10 | L2, U3 | brief | 6 | L3, U6 | **confine** | 9 | **L1, U10** |
| adjust | 5 | L4, U3 | bulk | 9 | L4, U9 | confirm | 7 | L4, U10 |
| **administrate** | 2 | **L1, U3** | | | | **conflict** | 5 | **L1, U2** |
| adult | 7 | L3, U6 | **capable** | 6 | **L1, U8** | conform | 8 | L4, U7 |
| **advocate** | 7 | **L1, U10** | capacity | 5 | L4, U9 | consent | 3 | L4, U7 |
| affect | 2 | L2, U6 | category | 2 | L4, U5 | consequent | 2 | L2, U3 |
| **aggregate** | 6 | **L1, U9** | cease | 9 | L4, U10 | considerable | 3 | L3, U8 |
| aid | 7 | L2, U7 | challenge | 5 | L3, U8 | consist | 1 | L4, U2, U9 |
| **albeit** | 10 | **L1, U7** | **channel** | 7 | **L1, U3** | constant | 3 | L4, U8 |
| allocate | 6 | L2, U6 | chapter | 2 | L3, U7 | **constitute** | 1 | **L1, U4** |
| **alter** | 5 | **L1, U1** | chart | 8 | L3, U10 | **constrain** | 3 | **L1, U8** |
| **alternative** | 3 | **L1, U10** | chemical | 7 | L2, U10 | construct | 2 | L3, U1 |
| **ambiguous** | 8 | **L1, U4** | circumstance | 3 | L2, U10 | **consult** | 5 | **L1, U6** |
| amend | 5 | L2, U9 | **cite** | 6 | L4, U10 | consume | 2 | L2, U2 |
| **analogy** | 9 | **L1, U4** | **civil** | 4 | **L1, U4** | contact | 5 | L2, U10 |
| analyze | 1 | L2, U3 | clarify | 8 | L4, U8 | **contemporary** | 8 | **L1, U7** |
| **annual** | 4 | **L1, U9** | classic | 7 | L3, U9 | **context** | 1 | **L1, U4** |
| anticipate | 9 | L2, U3 | clause | 5 | L2, U8 | contract | 1 | L3, U9 |
| apparent | 4 | L2, U9 | code | 4 | L4, U9 | contradict | 8 | L2, U2 |
| append | 8 | L2, U10 | coherent | 9 | L2, U5 | **contrary** | 7 | **L1, U6** |
| appreciate | 8 | L3, U5 | **coincide** | 9 | **L1, U5** | **contrast** | 4 | **L1, U7** |
| approach | 1 | L3, U1 | collapse | 10 | L4, U10 | **contribute** | 3 | **L1, U9** |
| **appropriate** | 2 | **L1, U8** | **colleague** | 10 | **L1, U5** | controversy | 9 | L2, U3 |
| approximate | 4 | L3, U4 | commence | 9 | L3, U9 | **convene** | 3 | **L1, U4** |
| arbitrary | 8 | L2, U8 | comment | 3 | L3, U3 | converse | 9 | L2, U8 |
| area | 1 | L4, U1 | commission | 2 | L3, U9 | convert | 7 | L2, U2 |
| aspect | 2 | L3, U4 | commit | 4 | L2, U6 | **convince** | 10 | **L1, U3** |
| assemble | 10 | L3, U10 | commodity | 8 | L4, U6 | **cooperate** | 6 | **L1, U2** |
| **assess** | 1 | **L1, U8** | communicate | 4 | L3, U2 | coordinate | 3 | L2, U6 |
| assign | 6 | L2, U9 | community | 2 | L2, U7 | core | 3 | L2, U5 |
| assist | 2 | L2, U5 | **compatible** | 9 | **L1, U9** | corporate | 3 | L2, U2 |
| assume | 1 | L2, U1 | compensate | 3 | L3, U4 | correspond | 3 | L3, U9 |
| assure | 9 | L3, U4 | compile | 10 | L2, U6 | couple | 7 | L3, U1 |
| attach | 6 | L3, U7 | **complement** | 8 | **L1, U7** | create | 1 | L2, U1 |

| Word | Sublist | Location | Word | Sublist | Location | Word | Sublist | Location |
|------|---------|----------|------|---------|----------|------|---------|----------|
| credit | 2 | L3, U6 | enable | 5 | L3, U10 | found | 9 | L4, U8 |
| criteria | 3 | L3, U3 | encounter | 10 | L3, U5 | foundation | 7 | L4, U4 |
| crucial | 8 | L3, U10 | energy | 5 | L2, U5 | **framework** | **3** | **L1, U1** |
| culture | 2 | L4, U10 | enforce | 5 | L4, U7 | function | 1 | L3, U1 |
| currency | 8 | L3, U9 | enhance | 6 | L3, U1 | fund | 3 | L3, U3 |
| cycle | 4 | L4, U5 | enormous | 10 | L3, U8 | fundamental | 5 | L4, U4 |
| | | | ensure | 3 | L2, U5 | furthermore | 6 | L4, U9 |
| data | 1 | L2, U3 | entity | 5 | L4, U5 | | | |
| debate | 4 | L2, U4 | environment | 1 | L2, U1; | gender | 6 | L2, U8 |
| **decade** | **7** | **L1, U7** | | | L3, U8 | **generate** | **5** | **L1, U5** |
| **decline** | **5** | **L1, U2** | equate | 2 | L2, U2 | **generation** | **5** | **L1, U7** |
| deduce | 3 | L4, U7 | equip | 7 | L2, U3 | globe | 7 | L3, U2 |
| define | 1 | L3, U2 | equivalent | 5 | L3, U10 | goal | 4 | L3, U3 |
| definite | 7 | L3, U4 | **erode** | **9** | **L1, U9** | **grade** | **7** | **L1, U7** |
| **demonstrate** | **3** | **L1, U5** | **error** | **4** | **L1, U10** | grant | 4 | L2, U9 |
| denote | 8 | L4, U6 | **establish** | **1** | **L1, U6** | guarantee | 7 | L2, U8 |
| deny | 7 | L4, U10 | estate | 6 | L4, U6 | guideline | 8 | L3, U3 |
| depress | 10 | L2, U4 | estimate | 1 | L2, U10 | | | |
| derive | 1 | L4, U10 | ethic | 9 | L2, U9 | hence | 4 | L3, U5 |
| **design** | **2** | **L1, U1** | ethnic | 4 | L2, U1; | hierarchy | 7 | L3, U4 |
| despite | 4 | L3, U2 | | | L3, U3 | highlight | 8 | L4, U3 |
| **detect** | **8** | **L1, U6** | **evaluate** | **2** | **L1, U10** | hypothesis | 4 | L4, U7 |
| deviate | 8 | L2, U8 | eventual | 8 | L4, U3 | | | |
| device | 9 | L2, U3 | evident | 1 | L4, U2 | identical | 7 | L4, U5 |
| devote | 9 | L3, U9 | evolve | 5 | L2, U7 | identify | 1 | L4, U2 |
| **differentiate** | **7** | **L1, U4** | exceed | 6 | L4, U1 | ideology | 7 | L4, U6 |
| dimension | 4 | L4, U5 | exclude | 3 | L4, U7 | ignorance | 6 | L2, U9 |
| diminish | 9 | L4, U4 | exhibit | 8 | L2, U5 | illustrate | 3 | L4, U9 |
| discrete | 5 | L2, U6 | **expand** | **5** | **L1, U7** | image | 5 | L3, U5 |
| **discriminate** | **6** | **L1, U10** | expert | 6 | L3, U8 | immigrate | 3 | L2, U1 |
| displace | 8 | L2, U7 | **explicit** | **6** | **L1, U3** | **impact** | **2** | **L1, U9** |
| display | 6 | L3, U5 | **exploit** | **8** | **L1, U5** | **implement** | **4** | **L1, U2** |
| dispose | 7 | L4, U6 | **export** | **1** | **L1, U3** | implicate | 4 | L4, U7 |
| distinct | 2 | L3, U7 | expose | 5 | L3, U5 | **implicit** | **8** | **L1, U3** |
| distort | 9 | L3, U6 | external | 5 | L2, U10 | imply | 3 | L4, U7 |
| distribute | 1 | L4, U8 | extract | 7 | L3, U2 | **impose** | **4** | **L1, U10** |
| diverse | 6 | L2, U8 | | | | **incentive** | **6** | **L1, U10** |
| document | 3 | L4, U9 | facilitate | 5 | L4, U1 | incidence | 6 | L3, U10 |
| domain | 6 | L2, U8 | factor | 1 | L3, U8 | **incline** | **10** | **L1, U7** |
| **domestic** | **4** | **L1, U3** | feature | 2 | L4, U1 | **income** | **1** | **L1, U3** |
| **dominate** | **3** | **L1, U5** | federal | 6 | L2, U3 | incorporate | 6 | L4, U4 |
| draft | 5 | L3, U6 | **fee** | **6** | **L1, U1** | **index** | **6** | **L1, U4** |
| drama | 8 | L3, U5 | file | 7 | L4, U6 | indicate | 1 | L2, U4 |
| duration | 9 | L4, U1 | final | 2 | L4, U3 | **individual** | **1** | **L1, U1** |
| **dynamic** | **7** | **L1, U5** | finance | 1 | L2, U2 | induce | 8 | L3, U7 |
| | | | **finite** | **7** | **L1, U9** | inevitable | 8 | L2, U8 |
| **economy** | **1** | **L1, U7** | flexible | 6 | L3, U9 | **infer** | **7** | **L1, U8** |
| edit | 6 | L4, U8 | fluctuate | 8 | L2, U7 | infrastructure | 8 | L4, U6 |
| element | 2 | L4, U1 | focus | 2 | L3, U8 | **inherent** | **9** | **L1, U1** |
| eliminate | 7 | L2, U9 | format | 9 | L4, U8 | **inhibit** | **6** | **L1, U5** |
| emerge | 4 | L2, U1 | formula | 1 | L4, U8 | initial | 3 | L3, U7 |
| emphasis | 3 | L2, U9 | forthcoming | 10 | L4, U3 | initiate | 6 | L2, U10 |
| empirical | 7 | L3, U4 | | | | **injure** | **2** | **L1, U1** |

| Word | Sublist | Location |
|------|---------|----------|
| innovate | 7 | **L1, U3** |
| input | 6 | L3, U6 |
| insert | 7 | L2, U9 |
| insight | 9 | L3, U7 |
| inspect | 8 | L3, U3 |
| **instance** | 3 | **L1, U6** |
| institute | 2 | L2, U8 |
| instruct | 6 | L4, U2 |
| **integral** | 9 | **L1, U4** |
| integrate | 4 | L2, U7 |
| integrity | 10 | L3, U7 |
| intelligence | 6 | L3, U8 |
| **intense** | 8 | **L1, U2** |
| **interact** | 3 | **L1, U8** |
| intermediate | 9 | L2, U7 |
| internal | 4 | L3, U7 |
| interpret | 1 | L3, U3 |
| interval | 6 | L2, U5 |
| intervene | 7 | L2, U8 |
| intrinsic | 10 | L4, U4 |
| invest | 2 | L2, U4 |
| investigate | 4 | L4, U8 |
| **invoke** | 10 | **L1, U3** |
| involve | 1 | L2, U3 |
| isolate | 7 | L3, U4 |
| issue | 1 | L4, U2 |
| item | 2 | L3, U10 |
| | | |
| **job** | 4 | **L1, U1** |
| journal | 2 | L2, U6 |
| justify | 3 | L2, U3 |
| | | |
| label | 4 | L2, U2 |
| **labor** | 1 | **L1, U2** |
| layer | 3 | L3, U4 |
| lecture | 6 | L4, U2 |
| legal | 1 | L2, U3 |
| legislate | 1 | L3, U3 |
| levy | 10 | L2, U9 |
| liberal | 5 | L2, U1 |
| license | 5 | L3, U9 |
| likewise | 10 | L4, U5 |
| **link** | 3 | **L1, U8** |
| locate | 3 | L2, U1 |
| **logic** | 5 | **L1, U6** |
| | | |
| maintain | 2 | L4, U1 |
| major | 1 | L3, U2 |
| manipulate | 8 | L4, U4 |
| manual | 9 | L3, U10 |
| margin | 5 | L4, U3 |
| **mature** | 9 | **L1, U8** |
| maximize | 3 | L2, U8 |

| Word | Sublist | Location |
|------|---------|----------|
| mechanism | 4 | L3, U9 |
| **media** | 7 | **L1, U5** |
| mediate | 9 | L4, U2 |
| **medical** | 5 | **L1, U2** |
| medium | 9 | L2, U2 |
| mental | 5 | L2, U6 |
| method | 1 | L4, U9 |
| migrate | 6 | L3, U2 |
| **military** | 9 | **L1, U4** |
| minimal | 9 | L2, U10 |
| **minimize** | 8 | **L1, U1** |
| minimum | 6 | L4, U5 |
| **ministry** | 6 | **L1, U2** |
| minor | 3 | L3, U7 |
| mode | 7 | L4, U7 |
| modify | 5 | L2, U3 |
| monitor | 5 | L2, U3 |
| **motive** | 6 | **L1, U6** |
| mutual | 9 | L3, U3 |
| | | |
| negate | 3 | L4, U2 |
| network | 5 | L3, U2 |
| neutral | 6 | L2, U10 |
| nevertheless | 6 | L4, U10 |
| nonetheless | 10 | L4, U7 |
| norm | 9 | L4, U6 |
| normal | 2 | L3, U8; L4, U2 |
| notion | 5 | L4, U9 |
| notwithstanding | 10 | L2, U1 |
| nuclear | 8 | L2, U7 |
| | | |
| **objective** | 5 | **L1, U10** |
| obtain | 2 | L3, U6 |
| obvious | 4 | L3, U7 |
| **occupy** | 4 | **L1, U9** |
| **occur** | 1 | **L1, U2** |
| **odd** | 10 | **L1, U8** |
| offset | 8 | L4, U8 |
| ongoing | 10 | L3, U3 |
| option | 4 | L4, U7 |
| orient | 5 | L2, U5 |
| outcome | 3 | L3, U4 |
| **output** | 4 | **L1, U7** |
| overall | 4 | L2, U6 |
| **overlap** | 9 | **L1, U7** |
| **overseas** | 6 | **L1, U1** |
| | | |
| **panel** | 10 | **L1, U6** |
| paradigm | 7 | L2, U6 |
| paragraph | 8 | L3, U6 |
| parallel | 4 | L3, U9 |
| parameter | 4 | L4, U5 |

| Word | Sublist | Location |
|------|---------|----------|
| **participate** | 2 | **L1, U8** |
| partner | 3 | L3, U1 |
| passive | 9 | L2, U8 |
| perceive | 2 | L2, U9 |
| percent | 1 | L2, U10 |
| period | 1 | L2, U6 |
| persist | 10 | L2, U4 |
| perspective | 5 | L3, U2 |
| **phase** | 4 | **L1, U8** |
| phenomenon | 7 | L2, U5 |
| philosophy | 3 | L4, U5 |
| physical | 3 | L4, U4 |
| plus | 8 | L4, U5 |
| policy | 1 | L3, U3 |
| portion | 9 | L3, U9 |
| pose | 10 | L3, U1 |
| **positive** | 2 | **L1, U5** |
| potential | 2 | L4, U8 |
| **practitioner** | 8 | **L1, U2** |
| precede | 6 | L2, U4 |
| precise | 5 | L3, U10 |
| predict | 4 | L2, U1 |
| **predominant** | 8 | **L1, U8** |
| preliminary | 9 | L4, U1 |
| presume | 6 | L2, U2 |
| previous | 2 | L2, U5 |
| **primary** | 2 | **L1, U1** |
| prime | 5 | L4, U4 |
| principal | 4 | L4, U5 |
| principle | 1 | L3, U9 |
| prior | 4 | L3, U6 |
| **priority** | 7 | **L1, U2** |
| proceed | 1 | L4, U9 |
| **process** | 1 | **L1, U9** |
| **professional** | 4 | **L1, U5** |
| prohibit | 7 | L3, U10 |
| project | 4 | L4, U4,U9 |
| promote | 4 | L2, U6 |
| **proportion** | 3 | **L1, U10** |
| prospect | 8 | L2, U6 |
| protocol | 9 | L2, U4 |
| psychology | 5 | L4, U2 |
| publication | 7 | L3, U1 |
| **publish** | 3 | **L1, U3** |
| purchase | 2 | L2, U9 |
| pursue | 5 | L3, U8 |
| | | |
| qualitative | 9 | L3, U9 |
| quote | 7 | L4, U10 |
| | | |
| radical | 8 | L3, U4 |
| random | 8 | L2, U7 |
| range | 2 | L3, U1 |

| Word | Sublist | Location | Word | Sublist | Location | Word | Sublist | Location |
|---|---|---|---|---|---|---|---|---|
| **ratio** | 5 | **L1, U8** | so-called | 10 | L2, U8 | transport | 6 | L4, U10 |
| rational | 6 | L3, U3 | sole | 7 | L4, U1 | trend | 5 | L4, U6 |
| react | 3 | L2, U6 | **somewhat** | 7 | **L1, U4** | trigger | 9 | L3, U7 |
| recover | 6 | L3, U4 | source | 1 | L3, U2 | | | |
| refine | 9 | L4, U4 | **specific** | 1 | **L1, U6** | **ultimate** | 7 | **L1, U9** |
| regime | 4 | L2, U10 | specify | 3 | L4, U6 | undergo | 10 | L4, U1 |
| region | 2 | L3, U1 | sphere | 9 | L3, U7 | underlie | 6 | L4, U6 |
| register | 3 | L2, U2 | stable | 5 | L4, U5 | undertake | 4 | L2, U3 |
| regulate | 2 | L3, U6 | statistic | 4 | L4, U7 | uniform | 8 | L3, U1 |
| reinforce | 8 | L2, U5 | status | 4 | L3, U2 | unify | 9 | L4, U5 |
| **reject** | 5 | **L1, U7** | straightforward | 10 | L3, U4 | unique | 7 | L2, U1 |
| **relax** | 9 | **L1, U8** | strategy | 2 | L2, U5 | utilize | 6 | L3, U8 |
| release | 7 | L4, U1 | stress | 4 | L4, U4 | | | |
| relevant | 2 | L4, U8 | structure | 1 | L2, U1 | valid | 3 | L4, U10 |
| reluctance | 10 | L2, U4 | **style** | 5 | **L1, U4** | vary | 1 | L3, U10 |
| rely | 3 | L3, U2 | submit | 7 | L2, U9 | vehicle | 8 | L4, U3 |
| remove | 3 | L3, U2 | subordinate | 9 | L4, U3 | version | 5 | L3, U5 |
| require | 1 | L4, U2 | **subsequent** | 4 | **L1, U1** | **via** | 8 | **L1, U4** |
| research | 1 | L4, U2 | subsidy | 6 | L2, U2 | violate | 9 | L3, U6 |
| **reside** | 2 | **L1, U2** | **substitute** | 5 | **L1, U1** | virtual | 8 | L2, U10 |
| resolve | 4 | L3, U4 | successor | 7 | L2, U9 | visible | 7 | L3, U5 |
| resource | 2 | L3, U8 | sufficient | 3 | L2, U10 | vision | 9 | L4, U3 |
| respond | 1 | L4, U7 | **sum** | 4 | **L1, U10** | visual | 8 | L3, U7 |
| restore | 8 | L3, U5 | summary | 4 | L2, U10 | volume | 3 | L2, U4 |
| restrain | 9 | L2, U7 | supplement | 9 | L4, U10 | **voluntary** | 7 | **L1, U10** |
| restrict | 2 | L2, U9 | **survey** | 2 | **L1, U3** | welfare | 5 | L4, U1 |
| retain | 4 | L4, U3 | survive | 7 | L3, U2 | whereas | 5 | L4, U2 |
| reveal | 6 | L3, U8 | **suspend** | 9 | **L1, U10** | **whereby** | 10 | **L1, U4** |
| revenue | 5 | L2, U2 | sustain | 5 | L2, U4 | widespread | 8 | L4, U10 |
| reverse | 7 | L2, U7 | symbol | 5 | L2, U2 | | | |
| revise | 8 | L3, U6 | | | | | | |
| **revolution** | 9 | **L1, U1** | **tape** | 6 | **L1, U6** | | | |
| rigid | 9 | L2, U7 | target | 5 | L3, U10 | | | |
| **role** | 1 | **L1, U5** | **task** | 3 | **L1, U8** | | | |
| route | 9 | L2, U5 | team | 9 | L2, U6 | | | |
| | | | **technical** | 3 | **L1, U6** | | | |
| scenario | 9 | L3, U7 | technique | 3 | L2, U1 | | | |
| schedule | 8 | L4, U9 | technology | 3 | L3, U8 | | | |
| scheme | 3 | L4, U3 | **temporary** | 9 | **L1, U9** | | | |
| scope | 6 | L4, U8 | **tense** | 8 | **L1, U10** | | | |
| section | 1 | L2, U5 | **terminate** | 8 | **L1, U9** | | | |
| **sector** | 1 | **L1, U3** | text | 2 | L2, U4 | | | |
| secure | 2 | L4, U6 | theme | 8 | L2, U2 | | | |
| seek | 2 | L4, U3 | theory | 1 | L4, U4 | | | |
| select | 2 | L3, U1 | thereby | 8 | L4, U3 | | | |
| sequence | 3 | L3, U5 | thesis | 7 | L4, U7 | | | |
| series | 4 | L3, U5 | topic | 7 | L3, U3 | | | |
| **sex** | 3 | **L1, U3** | **trace** | 6 | **L1, U9** | | | |
| shift | 3 | L4, U9 | tradition | 2 | L3, U6 | | | |
| significant | 1 | L3, U10 | transfer | 2 | L4, U1 | | | |
| similar | 1 | L2, U1 | transform | 6 | L2, U7 | | | |
| simulate | 7 | L3, U1 | transit | 5 | L3, U5 | | | |
| **site** | 2 | **L1, U6** | transmit | 7 | L4, U4 | | | |

# Notes

# Notes

# Notes

# Installation Instructions

**Close all programs before installing Diploma.**

## Installing and opening Diploma using Windows

1. Insert the Diploma CD-ROM in your computer CD drive.

2. If your computer is configured to install CD-ROMs automatically,
   - the Diploma installation screen will appear
   - click the "Install Diploma" option and follow the instructions as they appear on screen
   - click "Exit" when you are done.

   If your computer is not configured to install CD-ROMs automatically,
   - run the Setup Program by clicking on Windows "Start" button
   - select the "Run" option
   - in the box marked "Open," type "D:\Setup\DiplomaSetup.exe" (where "D" is the letter for the CD drive)
   - click OK
   - follow the instructions in the Diploma installation wizard.

   The software will be installed on your hard drive. You will need to restart your computer at the end of the install.

3. To open Diploma,
   - click the "Start" button
   - select the "Programs" option
   - choose "Diploma 6"
   - select the question bank that you want to use.

## Installing and opening Diploma using Macintosh

1. Insert the Diploma CD-ROM in your computer CD drive.

2. A folder of the CD-ROM's contents should appear. If the folder doesn't appear, double-click the CD icon.

3. Double-click the "Diploma 6 for Mac OS X" icon. Follow the instructions as they appear on screen. The software will be installed on your hard drive.

4. To open Diploma,
   - double-click on your hard drive icon
   - open the "Applications" folder
   - locate the "Diploma 6" program
   - double-click it to launch Diploma
   - a window showing available question banks will appear.